THE LIFE OF JESUS

VOLUME 2

Narrative: H. M. Rasi
Illustration: Heber Pintos

The story of the life of Jesus, based on the narratives written by Matthew, Mark, Luke, and John.

Bible references for each episode appear as footnotes for further reading; they are also listed in the last pages of this volume.

Pacific Press Publishing Association
Boise, Idaho, U.S.A.
Oshawa, Ontario, Canada
Montemorelos, N. L., Mexico

All rights reserved. No part of this publication may be reproduced, stored in a retrieval system, or transmitted in any form or by any means, electronic, mechanical, photocopying, recording or otherwise, without the prior permission of the publishers.

Available also in Spanish—*La vida de Jesús*

Copyright © 1985
Pacific Press Publishing Association
Printed in United States of America

Library of Congress Cataloging in Publications Data

Rasi, H. M. (Humberto M.)
  The Life of Jesus

  1. Jesus Christ—Biography. 2. Christian biography—Palestine. 3. Bible stories, English—N. T. Gospels. I. Pintos, Heber. II. Title.
  BT301.2.R3413   1984   232.9'01   84-14788
  ISBN 0-8163-0602-8 (v. 2)

85 86 87 88 89 • 6 5 4 3 2 1

GOD IS A LOVING FATHER WHO IS WILLING TO PARDON MEN OF ALL KINDS OF SINS, EVEN THOSE WHO ATTACK HIS OWN SON.

BUT THOSE WHO REPEATEDLY OFFEND AND REJECT THE HOLY SPIRIT —WHO SPEAKS TO THEIR CONSCIENCE— WILL REACH A POINT WHERE GOD CAN NO LONGER FORGIVE THEM. THEY WILL BE LOST FOREVER!

MASTER, WE'D LIKE TO SEE YOU DO ANOTHER MIRACLE. THAT WAY WE CAN DECIDE IF YOU ARE REALLY THE MESSIAH.

ISN'T WHAT YOU HAVE SEEN TODAY ENOUGH?

SOME DAY YOU WILL WITNESS A MIRACLE LIKE THAT OF THE PROPHET JONAH. JUST AS HE REMAINED ALIVE AFTER BEING SWALLOWED BY A BIG FISH, SO THE SON OF GOD WILL COME BACK TO LIFE AFTER THREE DAYS IN THE HEART OF THE EARTH.

WORRIED ABOUT WHAT THEY HAVE HEARD ABOUT HIS ACTIVITIES, JESUS' FOUR OLDER BROTHERS —SONS OF JOSEPH— DECIDE TO GO TO SEE HIM.

MOTHER, WE MUST CONVINCE JESUS TO GIVE UP THE KIND OF LIFE HE IS LIVING.

YES, BUT HIS TEACHINGS ARE MAKING HIM AN ENEMY OF OUR RELIGIOUS LEADERS. WE FEAR FOR HIS LIFE!

WHY? HE IS ONLY HELPING OTHERS!

53 VISIT OF JESUS' MOTHER AND BROTHERS—MATTHEW 12:46-50; MARK 3:31-35; LUKE 8:19-21.

As dawn breaks, Jesus and the disciples find themselves near the opposite shore of the Sea of Galilee. They are approaching the territory of Gerasa.

They look forward to some rest away from the constant pressures of the crowds.

The disciples don't suspect that they are being watched by two sinister figures on the shore. They are two demoniacs who live in a cemetery like savages.

More than once the local authorities had handcuffed and chained them. But the demoniacs were so strong that they always broke free.

Day and night the demoniacs screamed among the tombs as they hurt themselves against the stones. They had often attacked travelers, making people afraid to go near the cemetery.

As soon as Jesus and the disciples land, they hear blood-curdling screams. Looking up, they see the savages wildly running toward them.

57 THE DEMONIACS OF GADARA—MATTHEW 8:28 TO 9:1; MARK 5:1-20; LUKE 8:26-39.

59 QUESTIONS ABOUT FASTING AND THE TRADITIONS—MATTHEW 9:14-17; MARK 2:18-22; LUKE 5:33-39.

[71] A DEAF-MUTE HEALED; OTHER MIRACLES IN DECAPOLIS—MATTHEW 15:29-31; MARK 7:31-37.
[72] FEEDING OF MORE THAN 4,000 PERSONS—MATTHEW 15:32-39; MARK 8:1-10.

74 THE BLIND MAN NEAR BETHSAIDA—MARK 8:22-26.

5 TRIP TO CAESAREA PHILIPPI; PETER'S GREAT CONFESSION—MATTHEW 16:13-28; MARK 8:27 TO 9:1; LUKE 9:18-27.

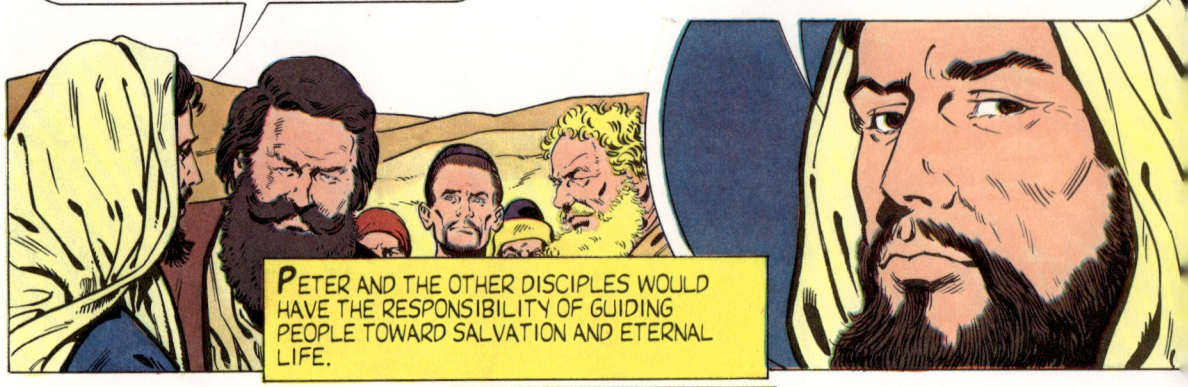

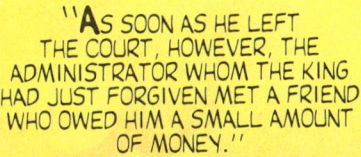

"As soon as he left the court, however, the administrator whom the king had just forgiven met a friend who owed him a small amount of money."

"He demanded the immediate payment of the debt, but his friend asked for a little more time to gather the money. Angered by this delay, the dishonest administrator grabbed him by the neck and told the guards to throw him in jail until the debt was paid."

"When the king learned of what had taken place, he summoned him to the court."

"There the dishonest administrator heard the king's words: 'You wicked man! I forgave you for your huge debt. Couldn't you have had compassion with your friend as I had with you?'"

My friends, this is how my heavenly Father will treat you if you don't sincerely forgive a brother who has done you wrong.

"Then he ordered him to be punished until he repaid all that he owed."

The Festival of Shelters was celebrated during early autumn. Pilgrims came to Jerusalem, built shelters out of branches, and lived in them for seven days. This festival reminded the people of how their ancestors had lived in tents in the desert during the Exodus. It was a happy occasion, with lights and music, that also marked the end of the harvest season.

In Jerusalem, some of the religious leaders are worried.

Be alert and report back to us as soon as any of you see Jesus of Nazareth.

There is no way we can allow him to speak in public here.

As the days go by, the expectation of the people increases. Will Jesus dare to come? How will his enemies react? Finally, midway through the feast...

Jesus is here! He's teaching in the temple. Tell everyone!

⌐ SECRET JOURNEY TO THE FESTIVAL OF SHELTERS—JOHN 7:2-13.

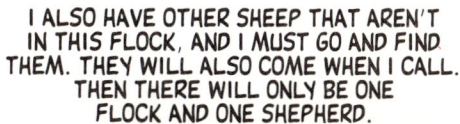

89 TESTS OF DISCIPLESHIP—LUKE 9:57-62.
90 MISSION OF THE SEVENTY—LUKE 10:1-24.

SOME TIME LATER THE SEVENTY RETURN, FULL OF JOY.

SIR, EVEN THE DEMONS OBEYED US WHEN WE USED YOUR NAME!

THAT IS GOOD NEWS BECAUSE IT SHOWS SATAN IS AN ENEMY ON THE RUN. I SAW HIM FALL LIKE LIGHTNING WHEN HE WAS EXPELLED FROM HEAVEN. AND SOMEDAY HE WILL BE DEFEATED FOREVER.

YOU MUST NOT, HOWEVER, BECOME PROUD BECAUSE YOU HAVE POWER OVER DEMONS. RATHER, BE HAPPY THAT YOUR NAMES ARE WRITTEN IN THE BOOK OF LIFE.

YOU ARE REALLY FORTUNATE! MANY PROPHETS AND KINGS OF LONG AGO WISHED THEY COULD HAVE SEEN AND HEARD WHAT YOU ARE EXPERIENCING TODAY.

ONE DAY, IN THE CITY OF JERICHO...

91

MASTER, WHAT MUST I DO TO HAVE ETERNAL LIFE?

WHAT DOES THE LAW SAY ABOUT THAT?

WELL, THE LAW SAYS, "LOVE THE LORD YOUR GOD WITH ALL YOUR HEART, WITH ALL YOUR SOUL, WITH ALL YOUR STRENGTH, AND WITH ALL YOUR MIND; AND LOVE YOUR NEIGHBOR AS MUCH AS YOURSELF."

RIGHT! DO THAT AND YOU SHALL HAVE ETERNAL LIFE.

BUT WHO IS MY NEIGHBOR?

LISTEN: NOT LONG AGO A JEW WAS TRAVELING DOWN THE ROAD WHEN SOME ROBBERS ATTACKED HIM.

"THEY BEAT HIM, STOLE HIS CLOTHES, AND LEFT HIM LYING HALF DEAD BESIDE THE ROAD."

PARABLE OF THE KIND SAMARITAN—LUKE 10:25-37.

92 IN THE HOME OF MARTHA, MARY, AND LAZARUS—LUKE 10:38-42.

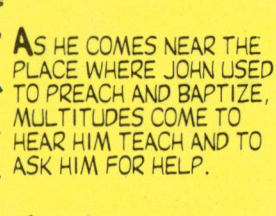

94 RETURN TO THE LAND EAST OF THE JORDAN; PARABLE OF THE FRIEND WHO CAME AT MIDNIGHT—LUKE 11:1-13; JOHN 10:40-42.

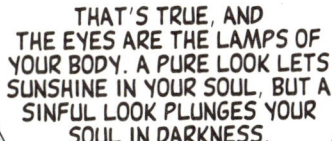

95 THE INNER LIGHT—LUKE 11:33-36.

96 DINING WITH A PHARISEE—LUKE 11:37-54.

97 WARNINGS AGAINST THE PHARISEES—LUKE 12:1-12.

175

"YOU STILL HAVE AN OPPORTUNITY TO RETURN TO GOD, BUT THERE ISN'T MUCH TIME LEFT.

"IT'S LIKE THE MAN WHO PLANTED A FIG TREE IN HIS ORCHARD AND WAITED THREE YEARS FOR FIGS. HE FINALLY DECIDED TO CUT IT DOWN."

"THE GARDENER, HOWEVER, ASKED THE OWNER OF THE ORCHARD TO GIVE THE TREE ANOTHER CHANCE."

SIR, LET'S GIVE IT ONE MORE YEAR. I'LL DIG AROUND IT AND PUT IN PLENTY OF FERTILIZER. IF THE TREE BEARS FRUIT, FINE; IF NOT, I'LL CUT IT DOWN.

IN THIS STORY THE FIG TREE REPRESENTS MAINLY THE NATION OF ISRAEL, WHICH FOR THREE YEARS HAD HEARD THE TEACHINGS OF JESUS.

ONE SABBATH, WHEN JESUS HAS FINISHED PREACHING IN A SYNAGOGUE IN PEREA, HE SEES A HANDICAPPED WOMAN WHO COULD NOT STAND UP STRAIGHT. HE APPROACHES HER.

101

WOMAN, GOD FREES YOU FROM YOUR SICKNESS THIS VERY MOMENT.

AREN'T THERE SIX DAYS TO WORK IN A WEEK? THOSE ARE THE DAYS TO COME FOR HEALING, NOT ON THE SEVENTH DAY!

HAVE YOU NO COMPASSION? YOU ALSO WORK ON THE SABBATH WHEN YOU UNTIE YOUR OX OR YOUR DONKEY SO THAT THEY CAN DRINK WATER!

SEEING THAT JESUS HAS HEALED ON THE SABBATH, THE LEADER OF THE SYNAGOGUE BECOMES ANGRY.

THEN WHAT IS WRONG WITH MY FREEING THIS POOR WOMAN WHO HAS BEEN HELD IN BONDAGE BY SATAN FOR EIGHTEEN YEARS?

MASTER, COULD YOU TELL US MORE ABOUT THE KINGDOM YOU SPEAK SO MUCH ABOUT?

102

WHEN GOD CREATED THE WORLD, HE SET ASIDE THE SEVENTH DAY TO REST, TO WORSHIP HIM, AND TO DO GOOD TO OTHERS.

HEALING OF A CRIPPLED WOMAN ON SABBATH—LUKE 13:10-17.
PARABLES ABOUT THE KINGDOM OF GOD—MATTHEW 13:31-33, 44-53; MARK 4:30-34; LUKE 13:18-30.

[103] SADNESS FOR THE FUTURE OF JERUSALEM—LUKE 13:31-35.   [104] DINING WITH A CHIEF PHARISEE—LUKE 14:1-14.

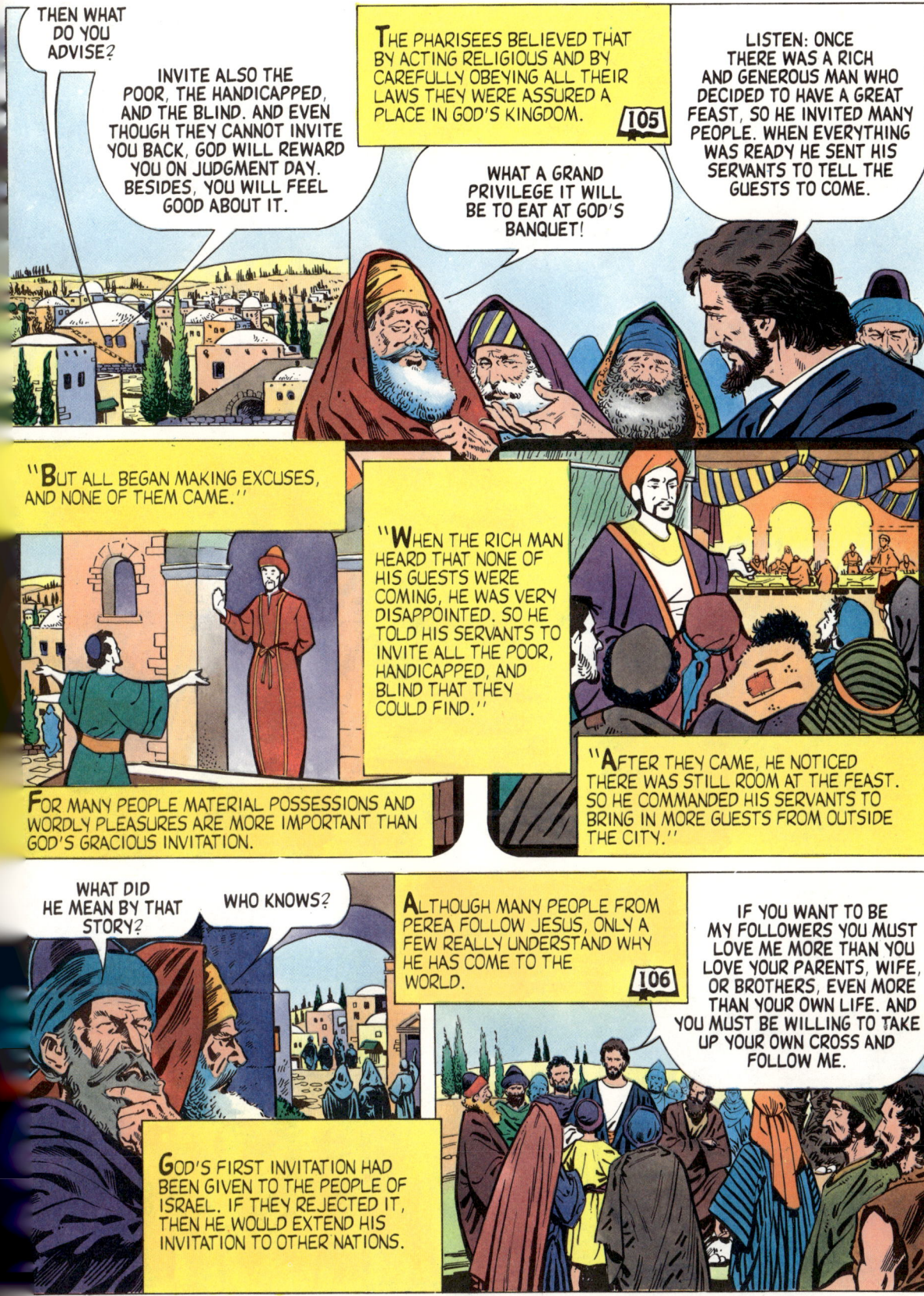

PARABLE OF THE LOST SHEEP—LUKE 15:1-7.

PARABLE OF THE DISHONEST MANAGER—LUKE 16:1-18.

14 THE SUPREME COUNCIL DECIDES TO KILL JESUS—JOHN 11:46-57.

PARABLE OF THE EVIL JUDGE AND THE PERSISTENT WIDOW—LUKE 18:1-8.

List of Episodes and Bible References

50. Second Galilean tour—Matthew 9:35; Luke 8:1-3. ... 97
51. The widow's son at Nain—Luke 7:11-17. ... 98
52. Healing of a blind and speechless demoniac; the unpardonable sin—Matthew 12:22-45; Mark 3:20-30; Luke 11:14-32. ... 99
53. Visit of Jesus' mother and brothers—Matthew 12:46-50; Mark 3:31-35; Luke 8:19-21. ... 101
54. Sermon from a boat—Matthew 13:1-9, 24-30; Mark 4:1-9, 21-34; Luke 8:4-8, 16-18. ... 103
55. Difficulties of being a disciple—Matthew 8:19-22. ... 105
56. The storm on the lake—Matthew 8:18, 23-27; 13:10-23, 36-43; Mark 4:10-20, 35-41; Luke 8:9-15, 22-25. ... 105
57. The demoniacs of Gadara—Matthew 8:28 to 9:1; Mark 5:1-20; Luke 8:26-39. ... 110
58. Matthew's feast—Matthew 9:10-13; Mark 2:15-17; Luke 5:29-32. ... 113
59. Questions about fasting and the traditions—Matthew 9:14-17; Mark 2:18-22; Luke 5:33-39. ... 114
60. The invalid woman; Jairus's daughter—Matthew 9:18-26; Mark 5:21-43; Luke 8:40-56. ... 115
61. The inquiry by the disciples of John the Baptist—Matthew 11:2-6; Luke 7:18-23. ... 119
62. Jesus' eulogy for John the Baptist; sadness for those who reject the gospel; an invitation to rest—Matthew 11:7-30; Luke 7:24-35. ... 122
63. Jesus instructs and sends the Twelve—Matthew 9:36 to 11:1; Mark 6:7-13; Luke 9:1-6. ... 125
64. Second rejection at Nazareth—Matthew 13:54-58; Mark 6:1-6. ... 128
65. Martyrdom of John the Baptist—Matthew 14:1-2, 6-12; Mark 6:14-29; Luke 9:7-9. ... 130
66. Feeding more than 5,000 people—Matthew 14:13-21; Mark 6:30-44; Luke 9:10-17; John 6:1-14. ... 133
67. Jesus walks on the lake—Matthew 14:22-36; Mark 6:45-56; John 6:15-24. ... 137
68. Discussion on the bread of life; rejection in Galilee—John 6:25 to 7:1. ... 140
69. Discussion about the religious traditions—Matthew 15:1-20; Mark 7:1-23. ... 142
70. Trip to Phoenicia—Matthew 15:21-28; Mark 7:24-30. ... 144
71. A deaf-mute healed; other miracles in Decapolis—Matthew 15:29-31; Mark 7:31-37. ... 146
72. Feeding of more than 4,000 people—Matthew 15:32-39; Mark 8:1-10. ... 146
73. The Pharisees and Sadducees demand a sign—Matthew 16:1-12; Mark 8:11-21. ... 147
74. The blind man near Bethsaida—Mark 8:22-26. ... 148
75. Trip to Caesarea Philippi; Peter's great confession—Matthew 16:13-28; Mark 8:27 to 9:1; Luke 9:18-27. ... 149
76. Secret journey through Galilee—Matthew 17:22, 23; Mark 9:30-32; Luke 9:43-45. ... 151